George Sewall Boutwell

The Reciprocity Treaty with Hawaii

Some Considerations Against its Abrogation

George Sewall Boutwell

The Reciprocity Treaty with Hawaii
Some Considerations Against its Abrogation

ISBN/EAN: 9783337226640

Printed in Europe, USA, Canada, Australia, Japan

Cover: Foto ©Suzi / pixelio.de

More available books at **www.hansebooks.com**

THE RECIPROCITY TREATY

HAWAII.

SOME CONSIDERATIONS

AGAINST ITS ABROGATION

WITH

OFFICIAL DOCUMENTS RELATING TO THE TREATY.

BY

GEO. S. BOUTWELL,
Counsel to Hawaiian Legation.

JUDD & DETWEILER, PRINTERS AND PUBLISHERS.
1886.

INDEX TO APPENDICES.

RECIPROCITY TREATY WITH HAWAII.

—

No measure ever had stronger or higher endorsement by statesmen of both political parties of the United States than the Reciprocity Treaty between Hawaii and the United States. It opened a very profitable trade to citizens of the United States, more particularly of California, creating a free market for productions and manufactures of the United States, ranking third in importance to the trade of San Francisco, leading to the building of between forty and fifty vessels, steam and sailing, in American ship-yards, and their constant employment till *one-fourth of all the arrivals and departures of vessels under the American flag in foreign trade to and from San Francisco are engaged in that trade.* It led to the building of large sugar refineries in San Francisco to supply the Pacific slope and contiguous territories with refined sugar, to a profitable investment of American capital in planting commercial, banking, and trading enterprises in Hawaii and California to an amount of over thirty millions of dollars, and all of this without injury to any other American interest. The amount of sugar upon which these enterprises depend—80,000 to 90,000 tons—does not amount to (7 %) seven per cent. of the consumption of the United States, and a commission of investigation have shown that 100,000 tons would be the maximum production of the islands.

The treaty gives profitable employment to the laboring classes in Hawaii, aids the prosperous development of that kingdom, makes permanent its political independence, and thus saves the United States from the serious complications which would arise from any attempt on the part of any other power to establish itself in those islands.

These results would not seem of themselves to constitute a valid reason for the abrogation of the treaty. But while the treaty could make possible these benefits, it could not regulate the distribution of the profits, which depended, as a matter of course, upon the enterprise, vigor, and perception of the individuals who first availed themselves of its advantages, and it was not provided that it should terminate for the reason that American citizens found it profitable.

The rivalries, jealousies, and sharp competitions of trade, however, have led to charges against and opposition to, the treaty itself which, though groundless and wrong, have once imposed on a committee of the House of Representatives. (See Appendix A.)

That committee, however, did not recommend abrogation, as it recognized the great national interests involved and the importance of the treaty to the country in the future development of the commerce of the Pacific. It only recommended investigation of the alleged "evils" to see if amendments were desirable.

An investigation was ordered by the Secretary of the Treasury, Hon. Chas. J. Folger, who appointed a commission of inquiry, which reported that the allegations against the treaty were groundless. (See Appendix B.) Mr. Folger, in his report as Secretary of the Treasury for 1883, alluded to the commission and its report which (see Appendix C), showed how the committee had been misled. The report was not regarded as wholly fair by Hawaiian officials, as is shown by a letter of the Hawaiian minister in transmitting it to his government, a part of which was published in the Hawaiian papers. (See Appendix D.)

The Secretary of the Treasury shows that many classes of American citizens are benefited by the treaty. It should be remembered that American goods are made free of duty in Hawaii by the treaty while goods of other nations are subject to duty. Allusion is made by him to a monopoly in sugar which then existed in California as not being a result of the treaty. That monopoly no longer exists; on the contrary, there is in San Francisco at the present time a "sugar war between the rival refineries, which has reduced the price of sugar to" a point cheaper than ever before.

Efforts are being again made to procure the abrogation of the treaty, and much stress is laid upon the loss of revenue to the United States, which is figured (at an exaggerated rate) upon the duties which would be leviable upon the grades and quantities of sugar imported under the present favorable conditions of trade. It would seem more fair to take, as a basis, the duties upon the grades and quantities which would probably be introduced if the treaty were abrogated. To claim that the same trade would exist without the advantages of the treaty would be to give away the case of the opposition by showing that there were no great advantages given by the treaty.

When the treaty was made the Secretary of the Treasury pointed out that the remission of duty would not occasion any *loss* of revenue, but that it would, to a small extent, reduce the *increase* of revenue growing out of the increased consumption of sugar. As a matter of fact, the entire importation of sugar rom Hawaii does not now amount to much over 15 per cent. of the *increase alone* in the consumption of the United States since the treaty was negotiated.

Of course the trade has grown. What else was expected when the treaty was made? Of course Hawaii has been benefited. What statesman would wish otherwise? If it had not, what profit would there be in trading with that country? But when complaint is made that the importations from Hawaii to the United States have increased fivefold, why not remember that the exports of the United States to Hawaii have also increased fivefold? If the United States has relinquished duties so also has Hawaii.

Much is said of the balance of trade. It has been said that the duties remitted equaled the cost of exports on the assumption that $3,000,000 in duties were remitted. No such sum is remitted (see Mr. Folger's report); and if it were, it is also true that the cost of carriage, the freights, commissions, insurance, and profits on the goods inure to citizens of the United States. What pays the cost of maintaining the commerce employed, interest on capital, &c.? Let one illustration show. The cost of rough lumber appears in the statistics at $8.00 per thousand ; it sells at Honolulu for $20.00 per thousand. That is to say, it takes in the ordinary course of trade $20.00 of imports of sugar to pay for $8.00 exports of lumber. The fact that many of the exports to Hawaii are bulky articles, such as lumber, hay, grain, agricultural implements, &c., is alluded to by Secretary Folger in his report. Let it be remembered that the duties collected in case the treaty should be abrogated would not necessarily nor probably equal the duties remitted. See also the letter of Secretary Frelinghuysen to the Committee on Foreign Relations of the Senate, Appendix E; and the report of Senate committee, Appendix F.

It has been said that the treaty brings the product of cheap labor into competition with American labor. As a matter of fact farm labor is as dear in Hawaii as in California or Louisiana; but how can competition be possible in sugar when all the sugar raised in Hawaii makes less than 7 per cent. of the importation into the United States? It is true that the Eastern refiner may claim that he meets the products of San Francisco refineries in the territories contiguous to California, but that is a natural and beneficial result of the competition of trade. The San Francisco refiner has free sugar from Hawaii. The Eastern refiner has all the free sugar of Louisiana and the benefit of the drawback on sugars exported, which, in 1885, amounted to twice the whole product of Hawaii. While the Eastern refiner has nine-tenths of the whole market of the country

to himself it would not seem too much to allow the Pacific slope t[h]
trade of Hawaii, which naturally belongs to it, if not drawn away
Australia or Canada by the abrogation of the treaty. The Paci[fic]
States have powerful rivals to contend with in competing for [the]
trade of the Pacific in Canada and Australia, and this treaty is[a]
great factor in the struggle.

Says the San Francisco *Commercial Herald and Market Review*
January 28, 1886:

Again, for the hundredth time, Hawaiian Reciprocity is threat[-]
ened, but we hope that in this the power of the General Govern[-]
ment will not be exercised to our detriment, as are the steamship
subsidy and silver questions. The trade with the Hawaiian Islands
has grown into gigantic proportions under the fostering influence
of this treaty; in fact it is, proportionately to the population of
the islands, the greatest trade that America enjoys with any foreign
nation, and in the sugar refining industry of this city it has developed one of the most prosperous manufacturing occupations in the
United States.

Already the line of American steamers built in Philadelphia to
run to Honolulu has extended its route to New Zealand, under a
subsidy from the government of that colony and of Hawaii. The
cable routes on the Pacific will centre at Honolulu, and the opening
of a ship canal or railway across the isthmus will inure largely to the
benefit of the country holding the commerce of those islands. What
considerations for abrogation are shown which are not dwarfed in
the minds of statesmen by such considerations as these? General
Garfield, in advocating the treaty, said : "Mr. Chairman, there are
two reasons why I specially desire the passage of this bill in relation to the treaty. The first is on the ground of the duty which the
nation owes to the Pacific coast; the second is on the ground of the
general good of the whole country. * * * If we do not make
this treaty schemes of annexation will vex us from year to year till
we shall be obliged to annex these islands as a matter of self-pro-
tection."

It is alleged that Hawaii is or will become a Chinese colony. The
fact is that the emigration of Chinese to Hawaii is forbidden by an
imperial edict by China, and their landing is restricted by law in
Hawaii. The Hawaiian government considers the present number
(17,000) as large as is consistent with its best interests, and immigra-
tion of other nationalities is encouraged.

It is not here intended to enter upon a discussion of the political
questions involved in the abrogation of the treaty. In the appendix

will be found some extracts upon the subject. (See Appendix G.) Suffice it to say that they are more important than they were when the treaty was made or when the committee of the House of Representatives reported that the political stipulations of the treaty were believed to be of "essential importance to this country."

The abrogation of the treaty would destroy a valuable trade and commerce built up under its guarantees by American energy, enterprise and capital, cause a loss of millions to American citizens, and open possibilities of evil results to both Hawaii and the United States. The amounts of money involved in the discussion of the treaty are insignificant compared with the political importance of the treaty, or the amounts which might be involved in case the islands are cast adrift to seek other alliances contrary to the interests of the United States and the security of the Pacific States.

Much is said of extending American commerce, and of maintaining the Monroe doctrine by the peaceful operations of trade—yet it is now proposed to abrogate a treaty which promises great commercial development in the future.

As it has been charged that the Hawaiian Islands have a system of peonage, an abstract of the laws of Hawaii and New York is added in Appendix II.

The United States having declared that it was its settled policy to exclude other nations from all interference in the affairs of Hawaii, could that position be maintained consistently after the abrogation of the treaty and Hawaii prevented from entering into reciprocal arrangements with Australia or Canada?

APPENDICES.

Treaty with Hawaiian Islands.

January 16, 1883, Mr. KASSON, from the Committee on Foreign Affairs, submitted the following report:

The Committee on Foreign Affairs, to whom was referred the bill (H. R. 2924) to terminate the convention or treaty of June 3, 1875, with His Majesty the King of the Hawaiian Islands, report herewith a substitute for the same, and recommend its adoption by the House.

The committee have heard somewhat voluminous arguments and many conflicting statements touching the facts involved with the question of the total abrogation or modification of the treaty of the United States with the Hawaiian government, which went into operation on the 9th of September, 1876. There are certain facts, however, which admit of no difference of opinion. The relative advantages to the people of the two countries appear to have essentially changed since the treaty went into effect. The change of these relations has been chiefly effected by the very large increase in the production of sugar and other products of the sugar-cane in the Hawaiian Islands, and which have been exported therefrom to the United States under the treaty in question. In round numbers the quantity of sugars so imported into this country free of duty, under the reciprocity clauses of the treaty, has increased from 30,000,000 pounds in 1877 to 106,000,000 pounds in 1882. It is alleged, and your committee is of opinion that it is truly alleged, that the intent of the treaty in this respect has been violated by the introduction of grades of sugar, under the Dutch standard of color, which are not within the description of the treaty, to wit: "Muscovado, brown, and all other unrefined sugar, meaning hereby the grades of sugar heretofore commonly imported from the Hawaiian Islands, and now (1875) known in the markets of San Francisco and Portland as Sandwich Island sugar, sirups of sugar-cane, melada, and molasses." This result has been accomplished by recent processes introduced for imparting an artificially debased color to the finer qualities of sugar, which render the Dutch standard no longer a just method for determining the quality and grade of the sugar imported. It appears that out of a total of 106,000,000 pounds coming to the Pacific coast from Hawaii in the last fiscal year 98,000,000 pounds came properly within the Dutch standard of numbers 10 and 16, inclusive, while in purity the average range is above 95 per cent. There is no question that this result is entirely without the intent of the contracting parties at the time the treaty was made. There can be also no question, therefore, that in this respect the treaty has ceased to be fair and reciprocal, and should be modified, or, in case that is impracticable, should be denounced under the right given to each government by its terms. There are also other modifications, which your committee believe it practicable to make, which will secure a more perfect reciprocity between the governments and the people of the two countries. The treaty, however, contains other stipulations in favor of the United States, the retention of which is believed to be of essential importance to this country. The effect of the treaty has already been to give to this Government the benefit of a satisfactory political influence with the government of the Hawaiian Islands, and to enable it in all cases to secure the just rights of its citizens who have already very large pecuniary interests in Hawaii. It is desirable to retain this condition as well with reference to our future as to our present national interests.

These islands are the nearest among the groups of the Pacific ocean to our western coast, and are the most important in their relations to our growing commerce with Asia and Australia. This commerce is only in the beginning of its development, and the Hawaiian Islands furnish a point on the route so valuable and so controlling that the traditional policy of this Government is firmly established against their domination by any foreign government, and against any undue influence exercised over the same, or acquisition of special rights therein, by any foreign power. Your committee believe that policy should be maintained, and that extraordinary measures on the part of our own Government to prevent such foreign domination might justly be taken. The treaty in question was made with a view to the maintenance of our influence there, and to the naval as well as commercial security of our interests in the Pacific. The situation of the United States gives to them a natural priority in the commerce between the American and Asiatic coasts. It would be folly to take any step which might lose to us the most important key to the commercial and naval situation. Without going further into the development of these considerations your committee are firmly of the conviction that the treaty should not be wholly abrogated, with the consequent loss of all its provisions for our rights and security, but rather that modifications should be introduced which shall obviate the evils which have given just grounds of complaint.

They therefore report to the House a resolution in accordance with the views above expressed, and recommend its passage.

APPENDIX B.

Report of Commission Appointed by the Secretary of the Treasury to Investigate Alleged Frauds under the Hawaiian Reciprocity Treaty.

WASHINGTON, D. C., *August* 29, 1883.

SIR: The undersigned, appointed by you a commission to investigate certain charges "made in Congress and in the public prints that, under color of the treaty between the United States and the Sandwich Islands, June 3, 1875, sugars have been imported from those islands into ports of the United States which were not entitled' to exemption from duty thereunder," respectfully submit the following report:

Upon receipt of your instructions, dated May 10, 1883, we proceeded directly to San Francisco and commenced the investigation in that city.

Upon examination of the report of the Committee on Foreign Affairs of the House of Representatives, dated January 16, 1883, and the "views of the minority" accompanying the same, dated January 29, 1883, together with "notes of hearings before said committee on the bill (H. R. 2924) to terminate the convention or treaty of June 3, 1875, with his Majesty the King of the Hawaiian Islands," and also the report on the same subject from the Committee on Finance of the Senate, dated February 27, 1883, we found the charges above referred to to consist mainly of two—

First. That the class of sugars imported since the treaty went into effect differs from that contemplated in the language of the treaty itself and from the importations from the Hawaiian Islands prior to said treaty; that, in fact, the process of manufacture in the islands had radically changed, vacuum-pans and centrifugals having been substituted for the open kettles and ordinary methods of purging muscavado sugars.

Second. That sugars from other countries were imported into the Sandwich Islands and fraudulently exported to the United States as Hawaiian sugars.

The treaty went into effect September 9, 1876, and is to remain in force for seven years from that date, "and further, until the expiration of twelve months after either of the high contracting parties shall give notice to the other of its wish to terminate the same."

It provides for the admission free of duty into the United States, among other articles grown and manufactured in the Hawaiian Islands, of "rice, * * * muscovado, brown, and all other unrefined sugar, meaning hereby the grades of sugar heretofore commonly imported from the Hawaiian Islands and now known in the markets of San Francisco and Portland as 'Sandwich Island sugar;' syrups of sugar-cane, melado, and molasses."

In the absence of samples of the sugars imported prior to the treaty, none of which appear to have been preserved, it was evident that the answer to so much of the first charge as relates to the class of sugars admitted was to be found mainly in the records of the custom-houses of San Francisco and Portland, and only to be ascertained by a careful comparison of the classifications of sugars imported from the islands during the years immediately preceding the treaty with those subsequently imported.

Inasmuch as the statistics of sugars imported from the islands heretofore made up and reported were based upon estimated classifications and not upon the appraiser's returns, the collectors of those ports, at our request, caused statements to be prepared from the invoices of each importation, showing the classification according to the appraiser's report and the number of pounds of each grade from July 1, 1873, to June 30, 1883, inclusive.

The work of compiling these statistics was done under our supervision, and we are satisfied that they furnish a true exhibit of the classifications.

From these statements we have made up the accompanying table (marked "A") which shows the quantity of each grade, the percentage of each for the several years, and the total quantity for the three years prior to and the seven years since the treaty, with the average percentage of each grade for the same periods. A second table (marked "B") shows the total invoice values of sugars imported each year, and the average value per pound prior to and since the treaty, together with the average and total amount of duties remitted thereunder.

These figures show a remarkable increase in the percentage of the lower grades imported into San Francisco from July 1, 1875, to September 9, 1876—while the treaty was pending—as compared with previous and subsequent years. During that period the proportion of sugars below No. 10, Dutch standard, was 62.53 per cent., against an average of the same grades of 15.28 per cent. in the fiscal years of 1874 and 1875, and an average of 14.52 per cent. from January 1, 1877, to June 30, 1883.

It appears that up to 1875 most of the better grades of Sandwich Island sugars were sold in the markets of the Pacific coast directly for consumption. Early in that year the San Francisco refiners made contracts to purchase the greater part of the crop of the islands, and arranged with the planters to make as large a proportion as possible dark in color, to meet the then-existing tariff. After the treaty was promulgated, the proportions of the several grades became about the same as before said arrangement was entered into. With this exception, it does not appear that there is any substantial difference in the character of the sugars imported prior to and since the treaty, nor is there any evidence that the importations under the treaty were not such sugars as were "commonly imported and known as Sandwich Island sugars" prior to 1876.

Information obtained from a large number of merchants and customs officials in San Francisco and Portland familiar with the subject was also to the effect that no material change had taken place in the character of the sugars imported.

It is worthy of notice that for the fiscal year ending June 30, 1883, there have been no importations at Portland of Sandwich Island sugar. It appeared from the statements of merchants in Portland that the direct trade between Portland and the islands, which before the treaty had supported regular lines of vessels, taking out assorted cargoes of merchandise and bringing back cargoes of sugar, (which was sold for direct consumption without refining,) has been broken up, the business being entirely controlled by the San Francisco refinery. Such vessels, being thus left without return freights, have been withdrawn, and direct shipments of American goods from Portland have been discontinued.

As the remaining charges could only be investigated satisfactorily in the islands, in accordance with telegraphic instructions, we proceeded to Honolulu, where we arrived on the 17th of June. A delay of a week in the sailing of the steamer shortened our stay in the islands to fifteen days, during which, however, we visited a large number of the sugar estates in the three Islands of Hawaii, Maui, and Kauai, and obtained, by actual inspection of the various mills, full information as to the character of the machinery in use, and, from the managers of the plantation, details as to the average yield of cane, possible increase of production, &c. We also saw the process of manufacture and the character of the sugar made, taking samples of the various grades. From data thus secured, which were also confirmed and completed by statements made by the agents in Honolulu of the various estates, we ascertained the following facts:

No *muscovado* sugar had been made in the islands for more than twenty years prior to the treaty. Centrifugals were manufactured and introduced in the islands as early as 1850 or 1851, and have been in use exclusively for purging sugars ever since that date. Vacuum-pans were also generally used as early as 1865, and in 1870 but few planters boiled their sugars in the open train. In 1875 there was but one, or possibly two, mills which retained the open train, and every mill started since that date has been equipped with vacuum-pans and centrifugals. The process of sugar-making is, therefore, unquestionably the same as prior to the treaty, and accounts for the fact, previously ascertained, that the quality of the sugars was substantially the same before as since the treaty.

The second charge made is, that sugars are imported from the East Indies and China into the Sandwich Islands, and thence reshipped to the United States as of Hawaiian growth and manufacture. This subject has been fully discussed by the American minister and United States consul at Honolulu, in reports of recent date, to which attention is called. After a thorough examination of the matter, we are convinced of the utter impracticability of such operations. The formation of the islands is such as in itself to forbid the successful smuggling of sugar. There is but one port in the kingdom where a vessel can lie with safety, viz., Honolulu. All the others are open roadsteads, at which landings must be made in boats, and at some of them this is attended with no little risk, even at the most favorable season. The landing of sugar at either of these ports in boats through the surf would be a tedious operation, and, from the nature of the coast, must be conducted by daylight. In a state of society such as exists on the islands, where every new arrival or unusual event attracts universal attention, the presence of a sugar-laden vessel and the landing of her cargo would of necessity involve such publicity as to preclude the possible success of the venture, to say nothing of the necessary after-handling and reshipment to the United States. This could only be accomplished by collusion between the shippers and the United States and Hawaiian officials, of which there is no evidence nor ground for suspicion.

It is a significant fact that, while vague charges of frauds of this nature are made, no specific case has ever been brought to the knowledge of either Government. The allegation seems to have no other foundation than the fact that there has been a large increase in the quantity of sugars sent to the United States since the treaty; but this increase can be otherwise accounted for. It is the legitimate result of the treaty itself.

The total imports of sugar from the Hawaiian Islands for the fiscal year ending June 30, 1875, according to table herewith, were 17,063,133 pounds, and from that date to September 9, 1876, when the treaty went into effect, 21,414,074 pounds. The quantity imported during the fiscal year ending June 30, 1883, was 115,325,077 pounds.

Immediately on the consummation of the treaty, which transferred the duty of fifty or sixty dollars per ton from the United States Treasury into the pockets of the planters, a great impetus was given to the sugar industry of the islands. The acreage of old plantations was at once increased and new plantations started. From statistics obtained in the islands it appears that three new plantations went into operation in 1875, five in 1876, eight in 1877, nine in 1878, eight in 1879, four in 1880, and one in 1882, bringing into cultivation over 20,000 acres of land additional, with a new capital investment of about ten million dollars.

The total yield of the several estates since the treaty corresponds with and accounts for the importations into the United States, as shown by the accompanying tables.

Among the papers referred to us in connection with the charges before named was a memorial of the eastern sugar refiners and merchants. A hearing was given to the representatives of the refiners of New York, Boston, and Philadelphia upon the allegations contained in said memorial. They presented no testimony, but rested their charges upon the language of the treaty itself, claiming " that it provides only for the admission of muscovado, brown, and unrefined sugars, whereas no muscovado sugars have been imported under the treaty, while large quantities have been received of what are known commercially as 'semi-refined' sugars, such as are, by reason of their color, fit for consumption without refining." They further claimed that " No. 13, Dutch standard, is the clearly-established dividing line between raw or unrefined and refined sugar, and that this principle was recognized by Congress in its recent legislation on the sugar tariff." In the absence of any knowledge of

Sandwich Island sugars in the eastern markets, the refiners and merchants were doubtless justified in the inference that the term "muscovado" was introduced because the islands produced drained sugars of this character. The non-importation under the treaty of this class of sugar naturally led to the belief that the process of manufacture had undergone a change. The fact is, however, as before stated, that for twenty years or more prior to the treaty no muscovado sugar had been made in the islands. Why the term "muscovado" was used we are not informed. It certainly had no place in the treaty, and has tended to mislead since, if not at the time of its adoption.

We took occasion while in the islands to procure from official sources accurate statistics and information on some minor points relating to the workings of the treaty, which have formed part of the discussion of these charges of fraud, and which appeared to us relevant to the subject under investigation.

One of the prominent points in this discussion has reference to the prospective large increase in the sugar production of the islands. There is, unquestionably, a large amount of arable land fit for sugar cultivation; but as, except upon the Island of Hawaii, the planters depend largely upon irrigation, the extent of the water supply fixes the limit of cultivation, which for this reason, it is estimated, cannot be increased beyond thirty to forty per cent. The yield per acre varies greatly, and is also largely controlled by the water supply. Some estates produced the past year five and a half tons per acre, while others yielded but two to two and a half tons, the average being probably less than three tons. It should be understood that it requires an average of eighteen months for cane to mature in the islands, and that not more than two-thirds of the acreage cultivated is cut in any one year. We are convinced that the output of all the islands, under the most favorable circumstances (unless by a better system of cultivation), would not exceed one hundred thousand tons of sugar per annum.

The rapid increase of sugar production created a corresponding demand for labor, which could only be met by drawing upon other countries. The laborers on the sugar plantations are native Hawaiians, Portuguese, Chinese, Germans, and Norwegians, with a few of the natives of the South Sea Islands and New Hebrides, and are generally esteemed in the order named. There having been no restriction upon the importation of the Chinese, the number of these who have come to the islands is greater than all other nationalities combined. The "Planters' Monthly," a magazine largely devoted to the consideration of the labor question in the islands, estimates the Chinese population in June, 1883, at 20,000. These are nearly all adult males, and outnumber the native population of the same class. We failed to find, however, any ground for the charges of ill-treatment of the laborers. Many of them, it is true, are imported under contracts running three or five years, but these contracts are fair to the laborer (see forms of contracts herewith, marked "G"), and are impartially enforced by the courts if violated. Official investigation of the condition and treatment of the laborers has been made by the German and Portuguese governments, with the finding that the laborer is well cared for and the contracts respected by the planters. It is certainly true that the laborers as a class are contented, and either renew their contracts or engage in day labor, with an assurance of steady employment, good treatment, and pay averaging from twenty-two to twenty-six dollars per month of twenty-six days of ten hours each.

Statistics furnished by the agents in Honolulu show that the greater part of the sugar machinery purchased for the islands since the treaty has not come from the United States, but from England and Scotland, or was manufactured in Honolulu.

The statement which has been frequently made that the greater proportion of the sugar planters are American citizens we found to be without foundation. Careful inquiry on this point regarding each of the estates on the islands shows that, aside from the Hawaiian Commercial and Sugar Company (a company organized in San Francisco), less than one-fourth of the owners of sugar estates and persons engaged in the sugar business are citizens of the United States. With a few exceptions, the business is in the hand of German and English citizens or Hawaiians. Among the latter are some who were born in the United States and have renounced allegiance to our Government, or who, born in the islands of American parentage, claim Hawaiian citizenship.

Conflicting statements having been made as to the relative values of imports into the island from the United States and other countries, we append a table (marked "F") compiled from the Hawaiian official records, showing the values of such imports for the years 1874 to 1882, inclusive, and the percentage of same from the United States.

It came to our notice during the investigation that American refined sugar consumed in the islands is manufactured of duty-paid raw sugar, and is exported from San Francisco to Honolulu with benefit of drawback. Thus, under the operation of the treaty and existing laws, the United States not only allows the Hawaiians the full amount of duty on the sugars they produced, but also on the American refined sugar they consume, such sugar being sold in Honolulu cheaper than in San Francisco.

The rice culture in the islands has been stimulated by the treaty even more than that of sugar. According to the Hawaiian official statistics (see Table C), the total exports of rice to the United States in 1873 were 892,720 pounds; in 1874, 885,646 pounds, and in 1875, 1,461,835 pounds. The admission of this staple into the United States free of duty has resulted in the increase of its production until, in 1882, according to the Hawaiian figures for the calendar year, there was exported to the United States 12,135,074 pounds, being the entire exports of rice from the islands, except 34,401 pounds, which went to other countries. The benefit of the duty remitted on rice goes almost entirely to the Chinese, who, either by purchase or lease of lands, have secured control of the rice cultivation.

It is charged that the treaty has created a sugar monopoly on the Pacific coast and increased the price to the consumer, but we did not find this statement warranted by the facts. It is true that the remission of the duty by the United States has not inured to the benefit of the consumer on the Pacific coast; but, as before stated, the duty, which, were there no treaty, would go into the United States Treasury, now goes to the planter, and not to the refiner who buys nearly the entire product of the islands. The increased cost to the consumer on that coast of refined sugars, as compared with the price paid by consumers in the Eastern States (from 2 to 2½ cents per pound), is not the result of the treaty, but grows out of a monopoly of the refining business in San Francisco, coupled with the still greater monopoly of railroad transportation.

In concluding this report, we desire to express our appreciation of the courtesies shown and assistance afforded us by Hawaiian officials, planters, merchants, and others in the prosecution of our inquiries.

We are also indebted to Mr. J. D. Power, of the special agent's office, San Francisco, who accompanied us to Honolulu, for valuable services rendered in the preparation of Hawaiian statistics while we were engaged in visiting the plantations upon the several islands.

Very respectfully,

O. L. SPAULDING.
JNO. E. SEARLES, JR.
A. K. TINGLE.

Hon. CHAS. J. FOLGER,
    Secretary of the Treasury.

APPENDIX C.

Report of the Secretary of the Treasury, 1883.

Charges of fraud and irregularity in the administration of the law enacted to carry out the treaty with Hawaii, so far as concerns the exemption of sugar from duty, having been made both in public bodies and public prints, I appointed a commission of three trustworthy persons (one of whom was nominated by prominent representatives of the sugar trade in New York) to go to San Francisco and Portland, Oregon, and, if necessary, to the Hawaiian Islands, to fully investigate the matter.

They were given the fullest latitude to examine into all branches of the subject, and have executed the commission with intelligence, fidelity, and thoroughness. Their report, which will be duly transmitted to Congress, fails to show that such charges have any foundation. It tends strongly to prove that the character of the sugar imported from these islands since the treaty went into operation is essentially the same as that which was imported prior to the treaty, both as regards the grade of sugar admitted and its country of origin, and that the treaty has been fairly executed. The statement in the report that the sugar interest is largely other than American has called forth from the Hawaiian government a counter-statement, with a table showing that of $15,886,800 of assessed plantation property over $10,000,000 is owned by American citizens. This large interest, it is claimed, is growth from the treaty, and that it is profitable to the owners, many of whom are residents in this country.

The industry and the free market opened have given rise to a trade, in its nature and effects, like our inter-State trade, covering a wide range of articles, affecting profitably the American farmer, grocer, and manufacturer of small articles of household and farm use, as well as the larger manufacturers in metals and of machinery and cottons. The exports in these commodities have so grown that the trade of San Francisco with the Hawaiian Islands is third in its importance, being equaled only by that with Great Britain and China, and exceeding that with Mexico, Australia, or British Colombia.

Many of the articles of this trade, such as hay, grain, lumber, &c., are so bulky that they employ a shipping large in proportion to their value, and much of this is American.

The impetus given to Hawaiian inter-island commerce has also inured to the benefit of Americans, in calling for coasting steamers and sailing vessels which have been built in American ports.

The balance of trade growing from the earnings of American commerce—the commissions of merchants and bankers and the profits of American citizens—is believed to be in favor of this country, as the course of exchange, as this Department is informed, is constantly against the Hawaiian remitter to the extent of from 1½ to 2 per cent. To reconcile this with the statements of the values of exports from this country to Hawaii, and of the imports into this country from that, which show an excess of imports, the fact must be weighed that the commodities landed there from here have an added value when they reach there from the cost of carriage which adheres to them. The carriage is by American vessels mostly, and the cost of carriage earned by our citizens should be put to that side of the account.

The report of the commission shows that but for the free entry awarded by the treaty the revenue on the sugar imported would have been about $3,000,000, computed at an average duty of $3.18 per 100 pounds.* Yet there is a countervailing benefit to our citizens. The increase in value of Hawaiian sugar has been but $1.57 per 100 pounds.

As the sugar comes in free it may not have been as strictly classified as that on which duty is assessed. That the consumer has received some benefit is thus shown, and this notion is confirmed by the market price of sugar in San Francisco before and since the treaty, being an average of 1½ cents per pound in favor of the consumer since the

---

* This amount is much exaggerated, being based on $3.18 per 100 pounds duty, which, on such sugars now (1886), would be about $1.80 per 100 pounds.

treaty. *Thus the loss of revenue is on a trade which might not exist but for the beneficent operations of the treaty.*

The portions of the report now italicised are worthy of particular attention.

APPENDIX D.

HAWAIIAN LEGATION,
WASHINGTON, *Sept.* 13, 1883.

SIR: I was to-day shown, through the courtesy of the Honorable Secretary of the Treasury, proof of the report of the commission to investigate the alleged frauds in the Hawaiian sugar trade. The report is both fair and unfair. It treats fairly of the questions of fraud and frankly states that the allegations are without any foundation in fact, either as regards the admixture of foreign sugars or the quality of Hawaiian sugars, but it dwells with peculiar unction upon the benefits the Hawaiian planter receives without making mention of the exemption from duty of American goods in Hawaiian ports. It states that the sugar consumer gets no benefit, but does not point out that the American producer and manufacturer does. The report seems to breathe a tone of lament that any advantages should have accrued to Hawaii in the bargain. It contains an apologetic explanation by the Eastern refiners as to how they came to make charges which proved so groundless, which, they say, came from the use of the word muscavado in the treaty. This I may say, from personal knowledge, was because it had been the term used in some other treaties or proposed treaties, and it was owing to the vagueness which had become attached to this term that the explanatory form or clause was added which really determined the grades intended. The report fairly and clearly disposes of the charge that the treaty is responsible for the high price of refined sugar on the Pacific coast, which it ascribes to a local monopoly and not to any effect of the treaty.

On the whole you will observe that the report is a manly admission that the alleged frauds did not exist, which is all the more creditable, as one of the commission had strenuously insisted that they did exist.

The statements in the report regarding the proportion of American citizens among the planters may be an unintentional error or may refer to the laborers. So far as the ownership of and capital employed in the sugar productions is concerned I think the report is wrong, and beg you to furnish me with late statistics touching this subject.

Had the commission, when it went beyond the questions of fraud to inquire into the benefits to Hawaiians of the treaty, also alluded to benefit to American commerce and trade, it would have made the report more comprehensive and satisfactory.

Appendix E.

Extracts from a Letter from the Late Secretary of State, Mr. Frelinghuysen, to the Chairman of the Committee on Foreign Relations of the U. S. Senate, of February 12th, 1885, on the Trade Relations of the United States with Several Countries on this Continent.

Your attention may be here invited to the working of the reciprocity treaty with Hawaii, which may be taken as illustrative of what similar treaties would effect in our trade relations with the so-called "inferior nations."

The trade between the United States and Hawaii in 1876 and in 1884 was as follows:

Years.	Exports to Hawaii.	Imports from Hawaii.	Totals.
1876	$809,000	$1,383,000	$2,192,000
1884	3,523,000	7,926,000	11,449,000
Increase	2,714,000	6,543,000	9,257,000

Of the total commerce between the United States and Hawaii during the year 1884 about 95 per cent. was effected in American vessels, showing that their trade, with all its profits, freights, insurance, commissions, &c., as well as the regular profits on the merchandise imported and the manufactures exported, is in American hands. In this connection it may be stated that the whole round of our trade relations presents no other such favorable conditions.

The latest Hawaiian returns at hand are for the calendar year 1883. According to these the total imports into the Kingdom amounted to $5,624,000. The imports of American goods admitted free under the reciprocity treaty amounted to $3,169,000.

The imports of Hawaii subject to duty amounted to $2,187,000, of which American goods constituted $813,000 and British goods $939,000.

The importation of free goods under the general treaty amounted to $267,000, in which American goods must have held their full share. It thus appears that out of a total import amounting to $5,624,000 American products and manufactures amount to $4,000,000.

The population of Hawaii is estimated at 70,000; our exports thither in 1884 amounted to $3,523,000; this shows a per capita consumption of American goods as they leave our ports of a fraction over $50.

The following statement shows the per capita consumption of American products and manufactures in the several countries on this continent, British North America excepted:

Countries.	Population.	Exports from the United States.	Amounts per capita.
Hawaii.	70,000	$3,523,000	$50 00
Mexico	9,300,000	12,744,000	1 36¼
Central America	2,660,000	3,608,000	1 36
United States of Colombia	3,000,000	6,380,000	2 09
Venezuela	2,075,000	2,427,000	1 17
The Guianas	295,320	2,306,000	7 82
Brazil	12,000,000	8,695,000	72¼
Uruguay	500,000	1,368,000	2 74
Argentine Republic	2,500,000	5,075,000	2 03
Chili	2,500,000	3,267,000	1 31
Bolivia	2,000,000		
Peru	2,700,000	1,071,000	40
Ecuador	1,000,000	629,000	63
Spanish West Indies	2,307,000	13,135,000	5 69
British West Indies	1,133,000	8,849,000	7 98½
French West Indies	384,000	1,821,000	4 75
Hayti	572,000	2,760,000	4 82
San Domingo	290,000	1,294,000	4 46
Total	45,216,320	75,389,000	1.668

In 1876 the consumption of American goods in Hawaii amounted to $12.66 per capita. The increase under the reciprocity treaty has, therefore, been $37.34 per capita.

It is not intended in this communication, even for illustrative purposes, to create the impression that any system of reciprocity treaties must produce such favorable results in the foregoing countries as has been produced in the case of Hawaii, although the stimulus which reciprocity treaties would give to the development of the resources of many of the smaller countries, and the consequent increase in the consumption of our products and manufactures, would, undoubtedly, result in a marked enlargement of the total volume of trade.

As in the case of Hawaii, our trade fostered and developed by reciprocity treaties would be largely in American hands, in the buying and selling, in the handling and shipping, as well as in the production and manufacture thereof—and it should be remembered that in international trade the handling, carrying, and shipping are secondary only to production, manufacture, and preparation—indeed, it may be questioned whether the commissionmen, handlers, and ocean carriers do not realize as much thereon as the producers.

Appendix F.

January 24, 1884, Mr. Morgan, from the Committee on Foreign Relations, submitted the following report:

The Committee on Foreign Relations, to whom was referred Senate joint resolution No. 27, "as to giving notice to terminate the convention of June 3, 1875, with His Majesty the King of the Hawaiian Islands," have had the same under consideration, and report the same back with the recommendation that the resolution be indefinitely postponed.

As the resolution invokes the action of the Senate to reverse, by the vote of a majority of the body, the solemn judgment of more than two-thirds of the Senate expressed with reference to this convention in 1875, the grounds on which this reversal is demanded require investigation.

A report from the Committee of Finance, made to the Senate on February 27, 1883, embodies the leading objections that have been urged to this convention.

The Committee on Foreign Relations, not being able to concur in the arguments stated or the conclusions reached in that report, state the following reasons in support of the opposite conclusions:

If it could be shown (as your committee have failed to discover that it has been) that the commerce or the revenues of the United States have not been adequately compensated by the advantages of actual trade with the Hawaiian Islands, under the convention of 1875, there are other and perhaps higher considerations than the relative money value of that trade to the people of the United States, which establish the wisdom of the Senate in ratifying and of Congress in legislating to carry into effect this convention.

Since the opening of the Suez canal the great commercial nations of Europe, notably England and France, have exhibited great energy and activity in building up trade and extending and consolidating their influence and power along the western shores of the Pacific Ocean and in the islands of the South Pacific. We have also extended our treaty relations to Corea, Siam, Persia, and Madagascar, with a view to a future profitable trade with all of the countries of Asia and Australasia.

Our transcontinental railroads have greatly increased our trade with all these countries, and have earned large sums of money in the transportation of mails and freights and passengers. When an isthmian canal shall have furnished quicker and cheaper carriage by steam vessels for freights and passengers, we will find powerful rivals in the field both by way of the Isthmus of Darien and at Puget Sound, in British Columbia. This competition will also extend along the coasts of Mexico and of the Central and South American States.

The stimulus thus given to commerce on the Pacific Ocean will increase rapidly the interchange of productions between all these great countries until that trade will equal, if it does not exceed, the value of the commerce across the Atlantic.

The Hawaiian Islands afford the only stopping place, in a distance of 20,000 miles, between our coasts and those of Japan, Corea, and China; and from Panama to the heart of those countries they are in almost the direct line of travel. They are east of the meridian which touches the western shore of Alaska, and may be said to be properly within the area of the physical and political geography of the United States. They are nearer to us than to any other great power.

Influences of a social and religious character, through which these islands were, in fact, opened up to modern civilization, have drawn those people closely to us, and they feel that they have greatly profited by the sympathy and consideration of the American people for their well-being as a nation. This feeling has been greatly strengthened since 1875. Our liberal reciprocity with them has confirmed a mutual feeling of regard, which has never been chilled by any unpleasant event.

Hawaiian trade, investment, population, and policy have been greatly influenced by the convention of 1875—so much so that almost every public act relating to commerce has direct reference to that treaty. American population there has increased considerably since 1875, and, of the entire value of sugar-lands in the islands, estimated at $15,886,800, as is shown in the letter of Mr. Daggett, our minister to that country, of October, 15, 1883 (which is herewith submitted), $10,235,464 belong to Americans. (See Appendix A.) These close and cordial relations between the people of the two countries, in respect to which the Governments also are in earnest sympathy, strongly forbid that we should abandon our reciprocal commerce, or avert our attention, or withdraw our sympathies from the Hawaiian people.

Whether in an honorable and peaceful rivalry for the commerce of the countries bordering on the Pacific Ocean, or in the protection of our commerce or our coasts in case of war with any great maritime power, our relations with the government of Hawaii, consistently with its independence and autonomy, could not become too intimate for our own welfare.

A single fact, of many, will suffice to illustrate this proposition. The kingdom of Hawaii is the only government in the North Pacific Ocean that is not a colonial dependence of some great power in Europe or Asia, and it is therefore the only neutral power in the North Pacific Ocean.

In the treaty of Washington, in 1871, the United States and Great Britain agree between themselves that as neutral powers they will not in future permit either belligerent to make use of their ports or waters as the base of naval operations against the other, or for the purpose of the renewal or augmentation of military supplies or arms, or the recruitment of men; and they agree to bring this rule, with others, to the knowledge of other maritime powers, and to invite them to accede to them. This law of neutrality we would be bound to enforce against the Hawaiian government in case of war between the United States and any maritime power; but, in doing so, we would deprive our war vessels of the right to take coal at the Hawaiian ports for a longer journey than 2,000 miles, while the ships of England or of any other European power would be entitled to take coal for a journey of 15,000 miles. This rule would permit them, in fact, to coal at Honolulu and harass our coasts and commerce with the greatest possible advantage, while it would cripple us essentially.

The supremacy of England or any great maritime power in the Hawaiian Islands would make of this rule, on which we in part relied for compensation in respect of the Alabama claims, a most formidable difficulty in the way of the defense of our Pacific coast and commerce.

The very liberal concessions made by the Hawaiian government in favor of our whalers and war ships, in article 7 of the treaty of 1849, followed by the agreement, in the treaty of 1875, that "the King will not lease or otherwise dispose of or create any lien upon any port, harbor, or other territory of his dominions, or grant any special privileges or rights of use therein, to any other power, state, or government, nor make any other treaty by which any other nation shall obtain the same privileges, relative to the admission of any articles free of duty, hereby secured to the United States," present the strongest possible evidences of good will towards us on the part of that government, and disclose its confident reliance on our protection against any serious aggression or disturbance from any foreign powers. These concessions have not been disputed by any power, and when we accepted them we also accepted the moral duty of an equivalent protection of the independence and security of that kingdom. This close relation of amity is, in relative degree, as necessary to our welfare as it is to that of the people of the Hawaiian Islands, and should be maintained in strict good faith.

The importance of the Hawaiian treaty, in its political bearings upon the United States, has been recognized by Presidents Tyler, Polk, Lincoln, Johnson, Grant, and Arthur, as indicated in messages to Congress. Our Secretaries of State have uniformly insisted, since the Hawaiian government assumed treaty relations with other countries, that the United States must stand in a nearer relation with that kingdom than any other nation can occupy.

The material advantages of the treaty of January, 1875, to the people of the United States consist in the furnishing of useful and lucrative employment to them, in increasing the supply and lessening the cost of many articles of general use, and enlarging the market and increasing the demand for their productions.

Under the first head, of furnishing lucrative employment to our people, the advantage has been very great.

Many Americans have gone to the Hawaiian Islands, and, with their industry, skill, and capital, have engaged in agriculture, mercantile pursuits, navigation, banking, printing, and many minor mechanical industries, from which they have realized fair returns. The transportation of articles of commerce has been chiefly carried on by Americans in American ships.

The statement of Mr. Daggett, already referred to, estimates the amount of American capital invested in the Hawaiian Islands in sugar production alone at $10,235,464 in 1883. Mr. Frederick H. Allen, former chargé d'affaires of the Hawaiian government, in a statement which has been presented to the committee, makes the following estimate of loans and investments by Americans, as they were in 1882, viz: $3,200,000 in ships and wharves, $3,300,000 in loans; and he mentions other lines of American steamers that were then about to be put into that trade, so that American capital to the extent of at least $20,000,000 has found profitable and permanent employment in the Hawaiian Islands since the treaty of 1875 went into effect. The interest and profit on this sum will average 10 per cent. per annum, yielding $2,000,000 to our people.

Since the treaty San Francisco is, practically, the only direct market for the productions of these islands. Mr. Comly, then our minister resident at Honolulu, writing to the Secretary of State on the 11th April, 1881, says:

The showing for American shipping is gratifying. Not only have our shipbuilders furnished nearly all the new steamers and other vessels introduced, and our owners also transferred most of the bottoms which have changed register to the Hawaiian flag under Hawaiian owners, but the bulk of all the trade between the two countries has been carried under the American flag. Excluding whalers, out of 235 merchant vessels and steamers visiting Hawaiian ports 179 were American, leaving 60 only of all other nations; total tonnage, 141,906; American, 99,619; all others, 42,302. These statements include also all Hawaiian vessels sailing, foreign. The Hawaiian flag covers coasting sail vessels, 42; steamers, 8; sailing, foreign, 14; tonnage, 10,148. Nearly all these vessels are of American build.

He writes again, June 6, 1881:

The influence of the reciprocity treaty upon the increase of our carrying trade between the Hawaiian Islands and the Pacific coast, and upon the still larger increase of our shipbuilding for Hawaiian owners, has been one of its most gratifying results. * * * Three years and a half ago, when I first reported for duty at this post, there was but one island steamer; now there are eight, and more ordered, every one of them but one American built. The increase in sailing vessels has been still larger. * * * It is but fair and just to admit that probably all this increased demand for American ships and shipbuilding grew out of the reciprocity treaty, and would never have existed except for its generative power. This generative power is reflex as well as direct. It creates a magnificent increase of island products; this creates. both demand and capacity for a large increase of the import trade from the United States; and these combined create the demand for carriers under the American flag, and for American factors, agents, bankers, insurers, and producers of almost every kind.

The trade with the islands is but a drop in the bucket. But compare the total amount of her exchanges between the Hawaiian Islands with those between all other countries and the United States; then apply to this last the same ratio of increase in our carrying trade and shipbuilding which we have gained here; the result, it seems to me, would show that, under like conditions of prosperity everywhere, all fear of the American flag disappearing from the sea might be abandoned. * * *

If our commercial policy with the Sandwich Islands is to be taken as only part of a great system intended to take in and bind together all the two great continents and their adjacent islands on our side of the world, it seems to me that there are such grand possibilities to the near future of the United States in such a scheme as would make the reciprocity treaty with these islands a conspicuous landmark in our commercial history.

The number of steamers running between the islands has increased since that date to ten or more.

The report of the Secretary of the Treasury for the year ending June 30, 1883, states that the total value of all imports into the

United States of articles free of duty was $206,913,289.47, and of this sum there were admitted free of duty from the Hawaiian Islands, under the treaty of 1875, imports to the value of $8,029,835.18.

Our exports to those islands for the same period were $3,811,913, of which $35,848 were coin and bullion, while our imports of coin and bullion were $42,847, showing nearly an equal export and import of coin and bullion.

There appears, therefore, an excess of imports over exports of $4,217,922.18. This is practically the sum that we admit free of duty from the Hawaiian Islands, the rest having been set off by the importation, free of duty, into that country.

The revenue on this small balance is an inconsiderable item when compared with the $206,913,298 of annual importations which we have put on our free list for the bettering of the condition of our people at large.

But this apparent balance in the exchange of commodities in substance represents only the profits and gains of our own people employed in agriculture, navigation, and in trade and financial dealings with the Hawaiian people.

The interest and profits on the $20,000,000 of investments in those islands, and in wharves and ships and loans, calculated at a rate lower than is in fact obtained, are $2,000,000. The freights, insurance, and handling of produce interchanged, mostly of heavy commodities, amounting in value to $11,841,748, at 10 per cent., which is far below the actual cost, are $1,184,174, and the commissions, earned almost exclusively by our own people, at 5 per cent., are $592,087.40, and, if the profits to our merchants are only 5 per cent., that sum is $592,087.40; in all, $4,368,348.

This is the actual state of trade, which accounts for the fact that with an apparent annual balance against us of over $4,000,000 we are not called upon to ship coin or to transmit exchange to Hawaii to pay it. It is paid to our own people. The reverse of this is true of our trade with England. During the last fiscal year the apparent difference in our favor between the value of exports and imports to England was $197,047,224; but England transported 85 per cent. of our commerce, and the freights, insurance, and other charges which we paid to her people reduced the actual balance of trade in our favor to less than $100,000,000. What we export to Hawaii is consumed there, and amounts to $45.44 per capita, while our imports from that country amount to 60 cents per capita of our population.

These advantages of trade, which we gain through our control of the commerce of these islands, are of much greater value to us than the amount of revenue we could have possibly collected on the goods admitted under this treaty free of duty. This trade, including exports and imports, was in 1875 $1,922,555. In the absence of the treaty there is no reasonable ground for supposing that it would have increased greatly, if at all; but in 1883 it has increased to $12,004,526, and the treaty is justly entitled to be credited with nearly the entire increase.

If we take the trade of 1883 as the basis on which to estimate the loss of revenue, instead of the trade of 1875, which would be about the true basis, still this loss of revenue enriches our own people, both because we are the creditor country and handle this commerce and because the taxes we remit are upon articles that are consumed by our own people.

If these islands furnish one-tenth of the sugar we consume, being admitted free of duty, it creates competition to that extent, which should correspondingly reduce the price. The necessity of reducing our present excessive revenues has earnestly engaged the attention of Congress for some time past, and if the entire customs duties which we could derive from articles of prime necessity imported from the Sandwich Islands should be remitted, the policy would be exactly in line with that which our redundant revenue is compelling us to adopt.

The most urgent complaints against this treaty are that it admits sugar and rice free of duty, these being productions that are grown to some extent in the United States.

A sufficient answer to these objections is found in the fact that there are no sugar or rice lands of any consequence in the United States west of the Rocky Mountains, and it is at least just to that important region that it should enjoy the means of obtaining these supplies on equal terms with the country east of those mountains.

The overland freights on Louisiana sugars exclude them from California and Oregon, and the Pacific States are therefore compelled to look to the Hawaiian Islands for their chief supply. Without this treaty they must import their sugars, under a heavy duty, from Hawaii, the nearest and cheapest market, and pay for them in money or in goods also taxed in that country, while the States east of the Rocky Mountains can exchange their untaxed commodities with Louisiana for all the sugar that State can produce.

Louisiana, in 1880, produced 171,706 hogsheads of sugar, and the other States 7,166; total, 178,872. In 1883 the entire sugar production from cane is estimated at 180,000 hogsheads, or 180,000,000 pounds, which is equal to about 3.25 pounds per capita. Add to this the importations from Hawaii, 106,181,858 pounds, and the total of untaxed cane sugar consumed by our people is 286,181,858 pounds. The amount per capita is 5.20 pounds. The per capita consumption of sugar in the United States is about 36 pounds, so that only one-seventh of the amount is on the footing of home production, for which we pay with our other productions. The other six-sevenths cost us $91,406,717, and the duty added of $46,172,378.85; total cost, $137,579,095.

To pay for this we send to Cuba $50,440,831 in money, that being the excess of our imports over our exports, and we send money in about the same proportion to all other sugar-producing countries.

The entire balance of trade against the United States in all the countries from which we imported sugar was, on the 30th of June, 1882, $113,674,356. Of this entire sum nothing was paid for with our own productions except $4,295,519, the balance in favor of Hawaii, and all of that was paid to our own people except $958,000, which was paid to Hawaii in foreign exchange bought from our bankers.

These statements establish the fact that, in proportion to its amount, the Hawaiian trade is far the most profitable that we have with any country.

In the report of the Committee on Finance to the Senate, made on the 27th February, 1883, complaint is made of violations of the Hawaiian treaty by the importations of sugars from other countries through that country, and that sugars have been fraudulently imported of higher grade than are described in the treaty as—

Muscovado, brown, and all other unrefined sugars commonly imported from the Hawaiian Islands and now (1875) known in the market of San Francisco and Portland as Sandwich Island sugars.

It is our fault, and not that of the treaty, if we permit it to be violated by our own officers in our own ports. But these accusations, whether against the Hawaiian Government or our own, have been thoroughly disproved by the report of the commission sent out to the Hawaiian Islands in May, 1883, by our Secretary of the Treasury. The sugar refiners of the Eastern States, who were most earnest in these complaints, selected one of the three members of that commission, and, as they all agreed in their report, it is presumably a full and fair statement of the facts.

As to the importation of sugar through the Hawaiian Islands from other countries the commission say:

After a thorough examination of the matter, we are convinced of the utter impracticability of such operations. The formation of the islands is such as in itself to forbid the successful smuggling of sugar.

The tables showing the quantities of sugar imported from the Hawaiian Islands, which accompany the report of the commissioners, establish the fact which they state, that—

It does not appear that there is any substantial difference in the character of the sugars imported prior to and since the treaty, nor is there any evidence that the importations under the treaty were not such sugars as were "commonly imported and known as Sandwich Island sugars" prior to 1876.

It is gratifying to find that our commissioners, after the most careful examination of the grounds of these complaints, both in our own custom-houses and in the islands, have been constrained to bear testimony to the honorable conduct of the Hawaiian government in the execution of the treaty of 1875.

The King of Hawaii has been earnest and faithful in his efforts to remove all embarrassments that have stood in the way of his treaty engagements with the United States. The remission of 15 per cent. of the duties fixed by the general tariff laws of Hawaii, to satisfy Great Britain, was a severe draft on the revenues of the kingdom. By this and other means our special treaty relations with Hawaii have been recognized as being rightful and satisfactory to other countries.

This kingdom, without any decided support from the United States, has vindicated the principles of the treaty of 1875 in the following article in her treaty with the German Empire of 19th September, 1879:

SEPARATE ARTICLE.

Certain relations of proximity and other considerations having rendered it important to the Hawaiian government to enter into mutual agreements with the Government of the United States of America, by a convention concluded at Washington the 30th day of January, 1875, the two high contracting parties have agreed: that the special advantages granted by said convention to the United States of America, in consideration of equivalent advantages, shall not in any case be invoked in favor of the relations sanctioned between the two high contracting parties by the present treaty.

More recently the Hawaiian government has made a treaty with Portugal containing a like declaration.

It sufficiently appears from the facts thus briefly presented in outline that to abrogate our treaty of 1875 the Hawaiian government would release these engagements with the other powers, and we would abandon the concessions of principles so favorable to us in respect of our peculiar political and commercial relations with the kingdom of Hawaii, which are now firmly established. We would thereby open the door to similar agreements between those countries and Hawaii, under which they would eagerly seize the advantages which we would throw away.

If we abandon the treaty we must also abandon the attitude we assumed when it was ratified, that our national interests are so identified with those of Hawaii that we cannot permit any other nation to gain such control in that country as will endanger our western coast, or seriously impede our commerce on the Pacific Ocean.

Australia is anxious to gain the trade we enjoy with Hawaii, and is but little further from those islands than we are. That continent of great islands needs the productions of Hawaii as much as we need them, and has many of the productions that we send to Hawaii.

The completion of the Canadian Pacific railroad from Lake Superior to Puget Sound would induce the Dominion of Canada to make most favorable terms with the Hawaiian government for the trade of those islands.

A canal through the Isthmus of Darien would cause the Hawaiian trade to seek better markets in Europe than we can offer for the purchase of the goods she needs; so that every new route of transportation leading to Europe will put in jeopardy our trade with the Hawaiian Islands, unless we continue and make permanent our existing treaty agreement.

Whatever objections have so far been found to the workings or the results of this treaty are greatly overbalanced by the advantages we have acquired in a national sense, and by the benefits to our people of a profitable trade with the Hawaiian people, and by the duty we owe the people of both countries to give certainty and permanence to the gratifying prosperity which this treaty has created.

APPENDIX A.

No. 92.] LEGATION OF THE UNITED STATES,
HONOLULU, *October* 13, 1883.

SIR: I have the honor to inclose herewith, from the Saturday Press of this date, a statement of the principal sugar plantations on the Hawaiian Islands, embracing their estimated value and the nationalities of their proprietors. It will be observed that of the sixty-nine plantations named forty-eight are credited mainly to American ownership, with a valuation of $10,235,464, out of an aggregate valuation of $15,886,800.

Very respectfully, your obedient servant,

ROLLIN M. DAGGETT.

Hon. FRED'K T. FRELINGHUYSEN,
Secretary of State.

[Inclosure in No. 92.—From the Saturday Press, October 13, 1883.]

Statement of Sugar Plantations on the Hawaiian Islands, 1883.

Name of plantation.	Value.	American.	British.	German.	Hawaiian.	Chinese.
Hawaiian Agricultural Company.....	$600,000	$565,000	$35,000			
Planting interests..................	150,000	50,000				$100,000
Halawa Sugar Company..................	100,000	98,000	2,000			
Planting interests..............	50,000	30,000	20,000			
Onomea Sugar Company.................	240,000	240,000				
Paukaa Sugar Company.................	170,000	170,000				
Honomu Sugar Company...............	200,000	110,100		$89,900		
Kaueohe Plantation..............	175,000	175,000				
Wailuku Sugar Company...............	360,000	324,750	4,500	3,750	$27,000	
East Maui Plantation.................	100,800	62,300	4,200	27,300	7,000	
Makee Sugar Company..................	500,000	500,000				
Kilauea Sugar Company.................	300,000	151,000	149,000			
Kealia Plantation	250,000	250,000				
Lihue Plantation................	600,000	428,514		171,486		
Planting interests..............	120,000	120,000				
Koloa Sugar Company.................	300,000	67,500		232,560		
Planting interests................	40,000	40,000				
Princeville Plantation...............	300,000	279,000			21,000	
Eleele Plantation.................	150,000		75,000	75,000		
Planting interests................	20,000			20,000		
Kekaha Plantation............	150,000	56,250		93,750		
Planting interests................	50,000			50,000		
Waialua Plantation,.................	150,000		150,000			
Waimanalo Sugar Company..........	216,000	74,500	6,000	12,360	123,140	
Olowalu Sugar Company..............	160,000		40,000	60,000	51,000	
Hitchcock, Brothers & Co.............	200,000	200,000				
Halku Sugar Company.	500,000	500,000				
Pepeekeo Plantation..............	400,000					400,000
Alexander & Baldwin	250,000	250,000				
Planting interests.................	100,000	100,000				
Kipahulu Plantation.................	125,000		125,800			
Planting interests................	100,000	67,000	33,000			
Ookala Sugar Company.................	250,000	50,000	175,000		24,000	
Kohala Sugar Company.................	500,000	449,000	51,000			
Pioneer Mill Company and planting interests..................	500,000	500,000				
Haua Plantation........................	250,000			*250,000		
Grove Ranch........................	200,000	183,250	4,250	12,000		
Waihee Sugar Company...............	250,000	250,000				
Makee Plantation	100,000	100,000				
Hawaiian Commercial Company.....	2,000,000	2,000,000				
Waikapu Plantation..................	250,000	125,000			125,000	
Hakalau Plantation	300,000	300,000				
Star Mill........................	200,000	150,000	50,000			
Hilea Sugar Company.................	300,000	240,000	60,000			
Naalehu Plantation..................	500,000	375,000	125,000			
Honokaa Sugar Company	200,000	26,000	94,000	80,000		
Planting interests.................	50,000	50,000				
Hawi Mill	150,000		150,000			
Planting interests................	150,000		150,000			
Union Mill	120,000		120,000			
Planting interests................	80,000		80,000			
Spencer's Plantation...................	200,000		200,000			
Paauhau Mill Company	200,000	100,000	100,000			

* 250,000, Danish.

Statement of Sugar Plantations, &c.—Continued.

Name of plantation.	Value.	American.	British.	German.	Hawaiian.	Chinese.
Planting interests	$100,000				$100,000	
Wainaku Plantation	75,000	$37,500	$37,500			
Pacific Sugar Company	100,000	39,000	25,000	$28,000	8,000	
W. Lidgate & Co	400,000		400,000			
Waiakea Plantation	160,000		160,000			
Hamakua Plantation	250,000		250,000			
Niulii Mill	80,000		80,000			
Planting Interests	50,000	20,000			30,000	
Moannii Plantation	60,000					$60,000
Kamaloo Plantation	50,000	50,000				
Meyer's Plantation	10,000			10,000		
Walanae Sugar Company	170,000	96,800	5,000	3,500	64,700	
Laie Plantation	75,000	75,000				
Heeia Sugar Company	200,000	100,000	100,000			
Reciprocity Sugar Company	80,000	10,000	10,000		60,000	
Huelo Plantation Mill and planting interests	150,000		100,000			50,000
Estimated value sugar interests in the kingdom	15,886,800	10,235,464	3,180,050	970,046	641,240	560,000

October, 1883.

Appendix G.

Political Value of the Hawaiian Treaty.

The peculiar interest of the people of the United States in the Hawaiian Islands dates back to 1820, when the first band of American missionaries went out to that then benighted country.

Through the unaided efforts of American missionaries the Government was brought up to a standard never reached by any other savage race, and by their advice and influence the rulers were restrained and guided in the right way until it became a constitutional monarchy in the family of nations. In the interim of passing from ignorance and idolatry to knowledge and Christianity, the islands were more than once threatened with and barely saved from the fate of so many of the Pacific groups. Both England and France viewed them with longing and jealous eye, and officials and subjects of both those countries tried to force the native King into committing some act which might be made an excuse for seizing the sovereignty. It was due to the vigilance and untiring energy of the men who composed that little band of American laborers in the cause of religion and civilization that the schemes and intrigues of these designing foreigners were baffled and brought to naught.

When, in 1839, the French required of the King a deposit of $20,000 as security for certain claims made by them, it was the American merchants who furnished the money, and thus prevented the seizure of the islands. And when, in 1843, Lord George Paulet, in command of Her British Majesty's frigate *Carysfort*, demanded a "voluntary" cession of the islands at his cannon's mouth, it was the sage advice and admirable diplomacy of Dr. Judd, an American missionary, which thwarted the object of the ambitious Englishman and saved the little kingdom.

A glance at the map of the North Pacific Ocean should be enough to convince any one of the political and commercial importance of these islands to the United States. If they were situated in the Atlantic as they are in the Pacific, and the center of political and commercial influences equally important to our Eastern coast, secured by a treaty that had been acquiesced in by the great European powers, would any American statesman propose to abrogate such treaty and cast them adrift because of the remission of duty upon fifty thousand tons of sugar per annum?

How much did it cost this country and prolong the civil war that Nassau and other islands in the Atlantic were under foreign control?

The growing importance of American commerce in the Pacific was well expressed by Mr. Seward in his speech in the Senate on that subject:

"Who does not see that henceforth, every year, European commerce, European politics, European thought, and European activity, although actually gaining greater force, and European connections, although actually becoming more intimate, will nevertheless ultimately sink in importance, while the Pacific Ocean, its shores, its islands, and the vast region beyond will become the chief theatre of events in the world's great hereafter."

This political importance has been conceded by the opponents as well as friends of the treaty. Hon. Philip A. Thomas, of Maryland, in a speech in opposition to the treaty, said:

"Great Britain, they say, will seize upon these islands if the treaty does not become the supreme law of the land." * * * "They forget that the 'Monroe Doctrine' is still extant in this Government, and that that doctrine will be enforced against Great Britain or any other power that may seize upon or attempt to hold these islands. If the presence of any one of them there should prove to be a standing menace to the vital interests of the United States on the Pacific coast, or if possession were held with hostile intent towards our country or its people, the policy of this Government, in such an emergency, was foreshadowed by Mr. Webster, as Secretary of State, in the administration of President Tyler, when, in reference to these very islands, he wrote that 'the Government of the United States would look with displeasure upon any effort of any other government to acquire any preponderating influence over the government of the Hawaiian Islands.' And, referring to the rumor then current that the French would probably take possession of the islands, he said that he 'trusted that they would not take possession, but if they did they would be dislodged if it took the whole power of the Government to do it.' Rest assured, Mr. Speaker," said Mr. Thomas, "that the same policy will be pursued whenever Great Britain or any other foreign government, with intent to destroy the peace or menace the interests of our Pacific States, shall undertake to assert dominion over the Sandwich Islands. They will be dislodged if it takes the whole power of the Government to do it."

Did the gentleman count the difference in cost between holding a position gained and in dislodging another from such a position? The *Virginius'* naval demonstration alone cost five millions of dollars. What would it have cost to dislodge Spain from Cuba?

The treaty was earnestly recommended by many of the officials of the United States who had represented their country at the islands, and by General Schofield, of the army, who had visited the islands, and made a careful examination of their position and condition, as will be seen by his letter, which is incorporated in the speech of Mr. Wood, chairman of the Committee on Ways and Means. He writes to the Hon. Mr. Luttrell, a member of the House, as follows:

"HEADQUARTERS MILITARY DIVISION OF THE PACIFIC,
"SAN FRANCISCO, CAL., *December* 30, 1875.

"DEAR SIR: Knowing your interest in the subject, I venture to give you my views in respect to the Hawaiian treaty, which is soon to come before Congress for legislative action.

"The Hawaiian Islands constitute the only natural outpost to the defenses of the Pacific coast.

"In the possession of a foreign naval power, in time of war, as a depot from which to fit out hostile expeditions against this coast and our commerce on the Pacific Ocean, they would afford the means of incalculable injury to the United States.

"If the absolute neutrality of the islands could always be insured, that would suffice; but they have not, and never can have the power to maintain their own neutrality, and now their necessities force them to seek alliance with some nation which can relieve their embarrassment.

"The British Empire, through its North Pacific and South Sea colonies, stands ready to enter into such an alliance, and thus complete its chain of naval stations from Australia to British Colombia. We cannot refuse the islands the little aid they need, and at the same time deny their right to seek it elsewhere. The time has come when we must secure forever the desired control over those islands, or let it pass into other hands.

"The financial interest to the United States involved in this treaty is very small, and if it were much greater it would still be insignificant when compared to the importance of such a military and naval station to the national security and welfare.

"I am, dear sir, yours, very truly,

"J. M. SCHOFIELD.

"HON. J. K. LUTTRELL, *M. C.*,
"*Washington, D. C.*

"Admiral Porter addresses a letter to the Hon. Mr. Wood, which is incorporated in his speech in support of the treaty, in which he fully sustains the views of General Schofield. The naval officers who have visited the islands have been in accord on the subject of intimate commercial relations with the islands, always bearing in view their future destiny.

"The London *Times* thus refers to a harbor at the islands:

"The maritime power which holds Pearl River Harbor, and moors her fleet there, holds the key of the North Pacific.

"Sir George Simpson, in his travels around the world, says:

"That this archipelago is far more valuable on this account that it neither is nor can ever be shared by a rival.

"These are the only islands which can form an outpost to the defenses of the Pacific States. There are no others. They have no rival; and in this consists their great value. They are totally unlike a single island in the West Indies as an outpost of defense.

" The following is an extract of the minority report of the Committee on Ways and Means, made in the House of Representatives on the Hawaiian treaty:

" Much stress is laid by the report of the majority upon the importance to the United States of obtaining a foothold upon these islands in the interests of our Pacific commerce with the continent of Asia, and of our safety in case of future wars with any great naval power.

" The undersigned are not insensible to these considerations. No European power should be permitted to obtain the sovereignty of the islands, or to gain such influence in them as to menace our security. To allow this would be contrary to the well-established canons of American policy, sanctioned by nearly a century of traditions and by the conceded maxims of international law. No European power can deny to us the peculiar right to exclude them from possessing what would be a standing menace of danger to us, and the possession of which, by us, would be no menace to them.

" The following extract from a recent report of Commodore R. W. Shufeldt, of the United States Navy, on the commercial importance of the Corea, present and future, in its relation to America, will be found to be of great interest:

" The acquisition of Alaska and the Aleutian Islands, the treaties with Japan, Sandwich Islands and Samoa, are only corollaries to the proposition that the Pacific Ocean is to become at no distant day the commercial domain of America. The Atlantic, either by force of circumstances or national indifference, has been given over to foreign flags, backed by the immense weight of European capital, but under natural laws the flow of commerce, as of emigration, is from the east toward the west, and the geographical position of the United States, in conformity with this law, points to the Pacific Ocean as the main highway of trade, and our country as the source from which the Oriental nations must obtain whatever they need in the way of commercial exchange. In all probability, within the next half century, the United States will find its largest market in Asia rather than Europe.

" The London *Times* of August 25, 1882, publishes a naval letter from Hong-Kong, under date of December 19, thus:

" It having been reported that a large extension of the Russian naval station was in progress at Vladivostock, the place has been visited by Vice-Admiral Willes, and what he there saw has apparently made so much impression upon him that a long dispatch has been transmitted to the admiralty upon the subject. A new dock for repairing ships and a slip for constructing small armed crafts are in hand. A factory for the manufacture of torpedoes and additional batteries to strengthen the defense of the place is employing several hundreds of hands in its construction. The Siberian flotilla, instead of comprising, as in the past, two aged schooners and three obsolete gun-vessels, now consists of two floating batteries, four schooners, and five gunboats of the newest description. For the moment Russia appears to have abandoned her hostile intentions upon Corea, but she seems to be none the less determined to constitute herself the leading naval power in the North Pacific.

" There are three powerful commercial nations that have large interests in the North Pacific besides the United States, viz., Great Britain, Russia, and China. France and Germany are a power in the South Pacific. Jarvis, the historian of Hawaii, says:

" That they hold the key of the Pacific Ocean, for no trade could prosper or even exist while a hostile power, possessing an active and powerful marine, should send out its cruisers to prey upon commerce; but once firmly established on them it might put at defiance any means of attack which could be brought to bear against them. Hence the commercial countries have been jealous lest some of them should have a superior influence.

"General Grant, in a letter from China, during his visit around the world, wrote:

" My belief is that in less time from now than half a century Europe will be complaining of the rapid advance of China.

❊ ❊ * * * * *

"President Lincoln, in reply to an accredited minister from Hawaii, said:

" In every light in which the State of the Hawaiian Islands can be contemplated, it is an object of profound interest for the United States. Virtually it was once a colony; it is now a near and intimate neighbor. It is a haven of shelter and refreshment for our merchants, fishermen, seamen, and other citizens, when on their lawful occasions they are navigating the Eastern seas and oceans. The people are free, and its laws, language, and religion are largely the fruits of our own teachings and examples.

But it may be argued that in face of the protest of the United States no nation would take possession or strive to acquire superior rights in the Hawaiian Islands.

Suppose the commercial supremacy which Australia was rapidly gaining in 1872-'3 had been permitted to go on unchecked by the treaty negotiated in 1874, and the islands had become as thoroughly Anglicized as they are now Americanized, with what grace could the United States have objected to British influence and control? Great Britain always contended that she did not desire to annex the Fiji Islands, but was compelled to do so to protect British commercial interests that had grown up spontaneously. And with how much less grace could the United States protest if they deliberately abrogate a treaty which has given form and shape to the policy insisted upon by American statesmen for forty years! Such an abrogation would be a virtual acknowledgment that the policy was deliberately abandoned, after which it would not lie in the mouth of the United States to protest against any other nation taking up what she had by a solemn act abandoned. Such a retreat from the position now gained, especially in view of the completion of an isthmian canal, would be paramount to an abandonment of any hopes of commercial supremacy in the Pacific.

If statesmen of the past had the prescience to foresee and claim for the United States the advantages lying in the control of this group of islands, with how much more emphasis should such control be claimed by statesmen in this day when a canal is being made by foreign capital which will *debouche* in the face of this group on which the commerce of the East, which seeks the canal, must rely for a port of supplies and repair!

No new treaty which now could be negotiated would be likely to receive the sanctions the present treaty has gained, and become a part of the international law regarding Hawaii.

Says the Oakland, California, Times, December 18, 1883:

" On our Atlantic coast all of the near lying islands are controlled by other governments. England dominates Jamaica and the Bahamas, Spain possesses Cuba, and Denmark St. Thomas, while Hayti is semi-barbarous. But on that coast our own Government is strong enough in equipment, fortification, and resources to be more indifferent to such environment than it can afford to be here. Driven out of friendly relations, which thrive on reciprocal trade with Hawaii, our coast line will be naked to the ocean and defenceless, with not a friendly port in the sea where an American ship can cast anchor.

 *   *   *   *   *   *   *

"The abrogation of the Hawaii treaty means the greatest contribution in our power to offer to England's monopoly of the traffic, the industry, the profits of the whole globe. We have stood guard over those islands while they underwent the pangs of transformaion from barbarism-to civilization. Commerce, under our protection, has transfigured them, and now they are in the last stage of development in which they approximate our features and take on the form of absolute assimilation, and we are asked to abandon them and drop the profitable and ripened results of a third of a century's care and culture into the waiting lap of England!

"The completion of the Canada Pacific railroad sharpens England's anxiety to supplant us in Hawaii. She covets the island trade for that Sound port which is to be the terminus of her Pacific road. She seeks near our shores a naval station where her war ships may shelter and her merchant marine find profit and protection.

"We have by wrong commercial policies abandoned the rest of the world to England. We have given over to her the seas where once we disputed her supremacy. Coast after coast and island after island has been nailed to her empire until she has coiled herself around the world like a serpent."

It may be asked, "How does this treaty secure to the United States these advantages?" The interpretation of treaties always involves something more than the meaning of particular and isolated articles and clauses. No statesman or diplomat can read this treaty without recognizing at once the force and effect, the scope and intent, of the treaty as a whole. It was more than a mere commercial treaty. It truly puts the commerce of the two countries on a satisfactory basis without embarrassing the revenue of Hawaii to too great an extent, and is and will be so long as the high tariff on sugar is retained somewhat favorable to Hawaii. If it were not so there would be no excuse for the fourth article, which applies only to Hawaii, restraining her from admitting free of duty the goods of other countries, or permitting any other country to get any territory or right to,use territory therein. It is this fact that Hawaii had a temporary advantage in the other articles of the treaty that gives the fourth article its great force. This article was not carelessly worded by the prudent and sagacious American statesman who framed it. It was not intended to be offensive to the Hawaiian king. Its effects were carefully calculated. . It was based upon the idea of interfering as little as possible with Hawaiian independence so long as that could be maintained, but providing for the direction in which the control of the islands should go when it was no longer possible to maintain it.

No greater testimony to the importance of the treaty could be given than that it was at once recognized by the quick appreciation of British, French, and German statesmen, who made strenuous protests against it, Great Britain going so far as to say to the Hawaiian government that they "could not allow" its provisions to come into force. The Hawaiian government was involved in a long and tedious diplomatic negotiation, extending over four years, with, however, very favorable results, Great Britain agreeing to the termination of one article of her treaty which was thought to be infringed, and Germany agreeing that so long as this treaty lasted she would not claim the same rights and privileges. It follows, therefore, that so long as this treaty lasts the superior rights of the United States have and enjoy the formal recognition of the powers—abrogate it and the powers would doubtless claim equal rights again. How far these governments were influenced in yielding to the diplomatic representations of Hawaiian statesmen by the hope that Congress would abrogate the treaty cannot be told; but that they would regard its abrogation as a great gain to them there is no doubt.

In the volume of Foreign Relations of the United States, of 1878, will be found an account of the difficulties met by the Hawaiian government. There is no doubt, however, of the scope and intent of the treaty in the minds of practiced diplomats.

Aside from this diplomatic view the treaty undoubtedly does foster the silent but potent forces which mould a nation and fix its destiny, as it was anticipated it would do. Read in the light of to-day the following remarks of Hon. Elijah Ward, of New York, in the Forty-fourth Congress, on the subject of the treaty, show a wise and far-seeing statesmanship as to how the treaty was to secure the advantages aimed at:

" Mr. Speaker : I have observed with much pleasure that the convention for the extension of the trade of the United States with the Hawaiian Islands was advised in the Senate by the triumphant majority of 51 against 12 votes, and has been sent to this House for its approval and appropriate legislation. It has become incumbent on Congress to do whatever is fairly in its power to open or extend markets abroad. This is one of the direct results which will be accomplished by the proposed treaty, and hence it should be supported by the representatives of the people without distinction of party.

* * * * * * * *

" The purchase of a preponderating interest in the Suez canal has justly been regarded as a masterpiece of statesmanship and far-seeing policy on the part of Great Britain. Its object is to maintain for that country its supremacy in oriental trade. I regard the treaty with the Hawaiian Islands as scarcely less important to our people than the control of the Suez canal is to British subjects. China and Japan are among the chief fields for our commercial and manufacturing enterprise, and it is of the utmost importance that we should possess adequate naval stations in the Pacific Ocean.

" For these reasons I regard the Hawaiian Islands, although no part of this continent, yet as commercially, politically, and in fact as part of its appurtenances, and to be properly included in the application of the Monroe doctrine, prohibiting the intervention of European powers in them. Of this it was well said by President Johnson in his message of December 5, 1865, that it has as law been ' sanctioned by time, and by its good results has approved itself to both continents.'

" It appears to me that however just and proper and gratifying to an honorable national pride the Monroe doctrine in itself may be, it is imperfect and little more than a barren ideality, unless, in an enlightened self-interest, we associate it with a friendly care for the commercial and material prosperity of the States we have so far taken under our protection. If we prohibit the interference of European nations with the States of this continent, shall we stop at that point and cultivate no further increase of friendly relations with them ?"

The activity of the partisans of British influence in the Hawaiian Islands to endeavor to induce the Hawaiian government to withdraw from its present engagements and accept the boon of cheap East India coolie labor (now denied them), under British protection, in place of the free market of America, shows that they still entertain hopes of the abrogation of the treaty, the importance of which British diplomats do not fail to see. *Apropos* of this the American minister, General Comly, reported in 1881, under date August 29, to the United States Government :

" I have had occasion formerly to report to the Secretary of State the discomfort felt by the British Commissioner and other residents here on account of the predominance of United States influence and interests in the Hawaiian Islands.

" The watchfulness of the Commissioner to find means of undermining this influence has been constant. *   *   *

" There has been a systematic and indomitable struggle to force the Hawaiian government into a convention for the importation of East India coolies, so as to give the English a separate judicature and furnish innumerable opportunities for meddlesome interference with the internal affairs of this Government."

This warning called forth from Secretary Blaine two dispatches, which laid down the position of the United States Government as follows :

In Dispatch of November 19, 1881.

*   *   *   *   *   *   *

" But if negotiations such as you describe are really in progress, you will ask for an interview with the Secretary for Foreign Affairs and make the following representation of the views of the United States :

" The Government of the United States has, with unvarying consistency, manifested respect for the Hawaiian Kingdom and an earnest desire for the welfare of its people." *   *   *

" The Government of the United States has always avowed, and now repeats, that under no circumstances will it permit the transfer of the territory or sovereignty of these islands to any of the great European powers. It is needless to restate the reasons upon which that determination rests. It is too obvious for argument that the possession of these islands by a great maritime power would not only be a dangerous diminution of the just and necessary influence of the United States in the waters of the Pacific, but, in case of international difficulty, it would be a positive threat to interests too large and important to be lightly risked." * * *

Again, more fully, under date of December 1, 1882 :

" Sir : My late instructions, and especially that of the 19th ult., will have shown you the deep interest with which the United States observes the course of events in the Hawaiian Islands. The apparent disposition to extend other influence therein on lines parallel to or offsetting our own must be watched with care and considerable firmness. The intelligent and suggestive character of your recent dispatches naturally leads me to a review of the relationship of the Hawaiian Kingdom to the United States at a somewhat greater length than was practicable in the limited scope of my instruction of November 19th. That dispatch was necessarily confined to the consideration of the immediate question of possible treaty engagements with Great Britain which would give to that power in Hawaii a degree of extra territory of jurisdiction inconsistent with the relations of the islands to other powers, and especially to the United States. With the abandonment of a feudal government by King Kamehameha III in 1839, and the inauguration of constitutional methods, the history of the political relations of Hawaii to the world at large may very properly be said to begin. The recognition of independent sovereignty by the great powers took place soon after, which act on the part of the United States dated from 1844. Even at that early day, before the United States had become a power on the Pacific coast, the commercial activity of our people was manifested in their intercourse with the Islands of Oceanica, of which the Hawaiian group is the northern extremity. In 1848 the treaty of Guadalupe Hidalgo confirmed the territorial extension of the United States to the Pacific, and gave to the Union a coast line on that ocean little inferior in extent and superior in natural wealth to the Atlantic seaboard of the original thirteen States. In 1848–49 the discoveries of gold in California laid the foundation of the marvelous development of the western coast, and that same year the necessities of our altered relationship to the Pacific Ocean found expression in a compromise treaty of friendship, commerce, and navigation with the sovereign King of Hawaii.

" Hawaiian interests must inevitably turn toward the United States in the future as the present as the natural and sole ally in conserving the dominion of both in the Pacific trade. This Government has on previous occasions been brought face to face with the question of a protectorate over the Hawaiian group. It has, as often as it arose, been set aside in the interest of such commercial union and such reciprocity benefits as would give Hawaii the highest advantages, and at the same time strengthen its independent existence as a sovereign State. In this I have summed up the whole disposition of the United States toward Hawaii in its proper condition. The policy of this country with regard to the Pacific is the natural complement of its Atlantic policy. The history of our European relations for fifty years shows the zealous concern with which the United States has guarded its control of the coast from foreign interference, and this without the extension of territorial possessions beyond the mainland. It has always been its aim to preserve the friendly neutrality of the adjacent States and insular possessions.

"The United States was one of the first among the great nations of the world to take active interest in upbuilding Hawaiian independence and the creation of political life for its people. It has consistently endeavored, and with success, to enlarge the material prosperity of Hawaii. On such an independent basis it proposes to be equally unremitting in its efforts hereafter to maintain and develop the advantages which accrued to Hawaii, and draw closer the ties which imperatively unite her to the great body of the American commonwealth. In this line of action the United States does its simple duty both to Hawaii and itself, and it cannot permit such obvious neglect of national interest as would be involved by silent acquiescence in any movement looking to a lessening of those amenities, and the substitution of alien and hostile interests. It firmly believes the position of the Hawaiian Islands, as a key to the dominion of the American Pacific, demands neutrality, to which end it will earnestly co-operate with the native government; and if, through any cause, the maintenance of such position, neutrality, should be found by Hawaii impracticable, this Government would then unhesitatingly meet the altered situation by seeking avowedly an American solution of the grave issues presented."

This latter exposition of the attitude of the United States towards Hawaii corresponds with the earlier announcement by Daniel Webster, quoted in the statement by Hon. E. H. Allen, and with the following extracts from the messages of Presidents Fillmore and Johnson :

Extract from President Fillmore's Message of December 2, 1851.

*　　*　　*　　*　　*　　*　　*

"It is earnestly to be hoped that the differences which have for some time past been pending between the government of the French Republic and that of the Sandwich Islands may be peaceably and durably adjusted, so as to secure the independence of these islands.

"Long before the events which have of late imparted so much importance to the possessions of the United States on the Pacific we acknowledged the independence of the Hawaiian government.

"This Government was first in taking that step, and several of the leading powers of Europe immediately followed. We were influenced in this measure by the existing and prospective importance of the islands as a place of refuge and refreshment for our vessels engaged in the whale fishery, and by the consideration that they lie in the course of the great trade which must at no distant day be carried on between the western coast of North America and Eastern Asia." * * *

Extract from President Johnson's Message of December 9, 1868.

* * * * * * *

"The attention of the Senate and of Congress is again respectfully invited to the treaty for the establishment of commercial reciprocity with the Hawaiian Kingdom, entered into last year, and already ratified by that government."

* * * * * * *

"It is known and felt by the Hawaiian government and people that their government and institutions are feeble and precarious; that the United States, being so near a neighbor, would be unwilling to see the islands pass under foreign control.

"Their prosperity is continually disturbed by expectations and alarms of unfriendly political proceedings, as well from the United States as from other foreign powers.

"A reciprocity treaty, while it could not materially diminish the revenues of the United States, would be a guaranty of the good will and forbearance of all nations, until the people of the islands shall of themselves, at no distant day, voluntarily apply for admission into the Union." * * *

There is probably little reason to fear that a policy of so long standing is to be abandoned, but there may be danger that the influence of sugar producers (who cannot be injured in the least by the importation of the amount of sugar raised on the Hawaiian Islands) may win votes enough to weaken the moral force of the treaty and keep alive the intrigues of those who seek to undermine the influence and interest of the United States in the Pacific.

Appendix H.

The following abstract of Hawaiian and New York laws will interest those who wish to see a comparison of the two codes:

HAWAIIAN LAW.	NEW YORK LAW.
Civil Code, § 1397.—All minors above the age of ten years may be bound as apprentices or servants; if females, to the age of 18 years, or to the time of their marriage with that age; or if males, to the age of 20 years, in manner following:	2 R. S., 3d ed., § 1, p. 215.—Every male infant and every unmarried female under the age of eighteen (18) years, with the consent of the persons or officers hereinafter mentioned, may, of his or her own free will, bind himself or herself, in writing, to serve as clerk, apprentice, or servant in any trade, profession, or employment, if a male, until the age
1. By the father of such minor, or if he be dead or be incompetent, &c., then—	of 21 years, and if a female until the age of 18 years, or for any shorter time, and such
2. By the mother, &c.	binding shall be as effectual as if *the infant*
3. By the guardian, &c.	*were of full age*, such consent must be given—
4. By the governor of the Island in which such minor may reside.	

Civil Code, § 1317.—Any person who has attained the age of twenty years may bind him or herself by written contract to serve another in any art, trade, profession, or other employment for any term not exceeding five years.

§ 1419.—If any person lawfully bound to service shall willfully absent himself from such service without the leave of his master, &c., he shall be compelled to serve not to exceed double the time of his absence, &c., &c., provided always that such additional service shall not extend beyond *one* year next after the end of the original term of service.

1872, Chapter XXXI.—"He shall be paid wages for such extra time at the rate stipulated for in the contract."

1876, amending § 1420.—If any such person shall refuse to serve, &c., masters may apply to any district or police justice, who may fine such offender not exceeding five dollars for the first offense, and for every subsequent offense not exceeding ten dollars; and in default of payment thereof such offender shall be imprisoned at hard labor until such fine with costs are paid.

1872, XXIV.—If any master shall be guilty of any cruelty, &c., or violation of any of the terms of the contract, &c., such person shall be discharged from all obligation of service, and the master shall be fined not less than five nor more than one hun lred dollars, and in default of payment thereof be *imprisoned at hard labor* until the same has been paid.

§ 1424.—No contract of service made in pursuance of sections 1417 and 1418 shall bind the servant after the death of the master.

1872, Chapter XXXI.—No contract of a married woman to serve another shall be valid in law, &c., and in case any woman contracts marriage while under contract to serve another, the marriage shall operate to annul said contract of service.

1. By the father of the infant. If he be dead, or be not in a legal capacity to give consent, then—
2. By the mother, &c.; then—
3. Then by the guardian, &c.; then
4. By the overseers of the poor or any two justices of the peace or any county judge of the county.

2 R. S., 3d ed., § 28.—If any person lawfully bound, &c., willfully absents himself without leave, he must serve double the time of such absence unless he shall otherwise make satisfaction, but such additional service cannot extend beyond *three* years next after the original term.

2 R. S., § 29.—If any person refuses to serve, any justice of the peace of the county, or the mayor, recorder, or any alderman of the city where he shall reside, has the power to commit him to jail.

2 R. S., § 30–32.—If any apprentice be guilty of any misdemeanor or ill behavior, or any master be guilty of any cruelty, &c., or of any violation of the terms of the indenture, complaint may be made to any two justices of the peace, or to the mayor, &c., who will summons the parties before them, and examine into the grounds of complaint, and if the same be well founded they may either commit the *apprentice* to solitary confinement in the common jail of the county for a term not exceeding one month, there to be employed at hard labor, or discharge the offending apprentice from his service and the master from his obligations; or, in case of ill-usage by the master, discharge the apprentice from his obligations of service.

2 R. S., 3d ed., §§ 21 and 42.—Upon the death of any master, &c., the executors or administrators may, with the consent of the person bound to service, signified in writing and acknowledged, &c., *assign the contract* of such service to another person. If the person so bound, &c., refuses to give such consent, such assignment may be made under the sanction of the court of sessions of the county, &c., and when so made will be as valid and effectual as if the consent had been given in the manner aforesaid.

It is evident from the above that the framers of Hawaiian labor laws were guided almost entirely by the New York laws in compiling them, and in many cases adopted the exact words.